A FRIEND IN THE LIBRARY

LIVING AND THINKING

BY

EVA MARCH TAPPAN

I0610391

British Library Cataloguing-in-Publication Data
A catalogue record for this book is available from the
British Library

LIVING AND THINKING

A FRIEND IN THE LIBRARY

A Practical Guide to the Writings of

RALPH WALDO EMERSON

NATHANIEL HAWTHORNE

HENRY WADSWORTH LONGFELLOW

JAMES RUSSELL LOWELL

JOHN GREENLEAF WHITTIER

OLIVER WENDELL HOLMES

IN TWELVE VOLUMES

VOLUME I

Eva March Tappan

Eva March Tappan was born on 26th December 1854 in Blackstone, Massachusetts, America. She is well known as a factual as well as fictional writer, but spent her early career as a teacher. Tappan was the only child of Reverend Edmund March Tappan and Lucretia Logée, and received her education at the esteemed Vassar College. This was a private coeducational liberal arts college, in the town of Poughkeepsie, New York, from which she graduated in 1875. Here, Tappan was a member of Phi Beta Kappa, the oldest honour society for the liberal arts and sciences, widely considered as the nations most prestigious society. She also edited the *Vassar Miscellany,* a college publication.

After leaving her early education, Tappan began teaching at Wheaton College, one of the oldest institutions of higher education for women in the United States, founded in 1834 and based in Norton, Massachusetts. She taught Latin and German here, from 1875 until 1880, before moving on to the Raymond Academy in Camden, New Jersey where she was associate Principal until 1894. Tappan also received a graduate degree in English Literature from the University of Pennsylvania. This allowed her to pursue her first love, that of reading and writing, and she taught as head of the English department at the English High School at Worcester, Massachusetts.

It was only after this date that Tappan began her literary career, writing about famous characters in history, often aimed at educating children in important historical themes and epochs. Some of her better known works include, *In the Days of William the Conqueror* (1901) and *In the Days of Queen Elizabeth* (1902), *The Out-of-Door Book* (1907), *When Knights Were Bold* (1911) and *The Little Book of the Flag* (1917). Tappan never married, being a happy singleton, and died on 29th January 1930, aged seventy-five.

INTRODUCTION

I HAVE sometimes wondered whether every one who owns the works of our great American authors realizes what a treasure he has, what a gold mine of pleasure and information. They are a library in themselves. If you would have history and biography, there is a generous supply of both, especially of poems and essays and sketches and stories about Americans and American history. There are good words on religious — not theological — subjects, sturdy and serviceable; on living and thinking, on nature, humor, travel, and home-life. There are stories short and stories long, there is the best American novel, and there are several others that have won fame and have deserved it. There is much on the subject of literature, particularly the literature of England. There are stories and poems that have been loved by the children — and the grown folk, too, for that matter — ever since they were published. There are letters and note-books, not dull, prosy ones, but bright, witty, entertaining productions that give us a better idea of the authors themselves than many a lengthy biography.

But these good things are hidden away between the covers of some fourscore volumes, and how is one to find them? It takes considerable courage to walk up to a "set" of books and decide blindly where to make the first attack. If some one could only be at hand to say, "You are interested in such and such a topic, and in volume two there is an exceedingly good poem on the subject"; or, "There is a story in volume six that you ought to read"; or, "I do not know anything else so practical and helpful as that essay in volume five," — then the attack would be easier. The little postern-gate in the walls of the fortress would have been opened, and you could make the stronghold your own.

But good friends are not always at hand when they are most wanted. That is why these little books have been written. Their object is to point out in a familiar way the great variety of subjects on which Emerson, Hawthorne, Holmes, Longfellow, Lowell, and Whittier have written, to give a little idea of what they have said on these subjects, and to tell where it may be found. I have not aimed at laying out a systematic "course of reading," but at being helpful in a most informal fashion, at being, as the title-page claims, "A Friend in the Library."

EVA MARCH TAPPAN.

WORCESTER, MASS., June 21, 1909.

LIVING AND THINKING

SOME high-school girls and boys were once reading Longfellow, and their teacher asked each of them to choose a poem to read aloud on the following day, giving a reason for the selection. Of course, there were two or three who thought that, because there was nothing that must be learned by heart, no preparation was needed. These read their "selections" with only slightly varying degrees of badness, and were evidently struggling hard to discover "reasons" as they went along. One was sure that he had a favorite poem, but, unluckily, he had forgotten which it was! The idler-in-chief declared that he thought "Driftwood" a most worthy poetical pro-

I

duction, and was unpleasantly surprised to learn that "Driftwood" was prose. These, however, were the excrescences, the hangers-on of the class. Nearly every one of the others made a good choice.

One young girl had been more conspicuous for the remarkable variety and gorgeousness of her dresses than for interest in her lessons, and the teacher expected her to choose either "Beware!" or "The Rainy Day" (i. 78). Behold, she read "A Psalm of Life" (i. 18); and as she read, she forgot the others, she remembered nothing but the poem; and she read it as if every word were a golden secret that she had just discovered. When she came to the end, her face was all aglow, and she exclaimed, "It is true, but I never thought of it before. It is wonderful. I did n't know there was such a poem in the world. Is n't this glorious!" and she read: —

> Not enjoyment, and not sorrow,
> Is our destined end or way;
> But to act, that each to-morrow
> Find us farther than to-day.

Some one has declared that each person has a keynote to which his whole being vibrates. This pretty butterfly of a girl soon passed from her teacher's ken; but I believe that in the old poem, so often repeated and parodied that one might have idly fancied all the virtue had long since gone out of it, she had found something that was to be a power in her life.

There is nothing like having a definite purpose. An arrow shot into the air may hit something, but it is decidedly more likely to hit if it is carefully aimed. A writer who is somewhat well known for his power of condensation has declared that it came from a remark of one of his college professors that words were expensive, and he was using far too many. He had then something definite to aim at, and he had hit the bull's-eye.

The first step toward getting a thing, either a bag of gold or a virtue, is to wish for it earnestly. The world may be, as the old verses used to say, a vale of disappointments; but the Fates are often kind, and what one longs for with his whole heart and mind and strength, he is reasonably sure of getting — provided his will does not wobble, and he is ready to pay the price. Longfellow's "Excelsior" (i. 88) contains the gist of the whole matter. If one's will never falters, he will achieve the mark which he sets before him;

but, like the Alpine climber of the poem, he
may have to risk danger and even the loss of
happiness. Emerson says ("Compensation,"
ii. 91), " 'What will you have?' quoth God;
'pay for it and take it.' " Elsewhere in the
same essay is his fine explanation of the
"dualism" which is in all things: —

For everything you have missed, you have
gained something else; and for everything you
gain, you lose something. If riches increase, they
are increased that use them. If the gatherer
gathers too much, Nature takes out of the man
what she puts into his chest; swells the estate, but
kills the owner.

Emerson's definition of real wealth is not
quite like that of the tax-lists. He says
("Manners," iii. 117): —

What is rich? Are you rich enough to help any-
body? to succor the unfashionable and the eccen-

tric? rich enough to . . . make the lame pauper
hunted by overseers from town to town, even the
poor insane or besotted wreck of man or woman,
feel the noble exception of your presence and your
house from the general bleakness and stoniness; to
make such feel that they were greeted with a voice
which made them both remember and hope? . . .
Without the rich heart, wealth is an ugly beggar.

One of the most valuable qualities of Emerson's essays is that they are so thoroughly
practical. They are not highly colored visions
of what might be; they take the world as it is
and suggest how to make the most of it. Here
is what he says of the man who thinks he can
gain something if he borrows or begs: —

Has a man gained anything who has received a
hundred favors and rendered none? Has he
gained by borrowing, through indolence or cun-
ning, his neighbor's wares, or houses, or money?
There arises on the deed the instant acknow-

ledgment of benefit on the one part and of debt on the other; that is, of superiority and inferiority. The transaction remains in the memory of himself and his neighbor; and every new transaction alters according to its nature their relation to each other. He may soon come to see that he had better have broken his own bones than to have ridden in his neighbor's coach, and that "the highest price he can pay for a thing is to ask for it."

In this essay Emerson gradually leads the way up to the noblest thought of all, to the losses which it seems impossible should ever bring any touch of gain, "a fever, a mutilation, a cruel disappointment, a loss of wealth, a loss of friends"; and he shows clearly and hopefully in his closing paragraph that from even these good may come, that character may grow and gain, that the "sunny garden flower" may become "the banian of the forest, yielding shade and fruit to wide neighborhoods of men."

Longfellow brings out a thought akin to this in his "Light of Stars" (i. 22) : —

> Oh, fear not in a world like this,
> And thou shalt know ere long,
> Know how sublime a thing it is
> To suffer and be strong.

Character is the greatest thing on earth. Emerson says in his essay on that subject (iii. 87) that character is reserved force, that in listening to a great man we always feel that there is something in him greater than his words. "We cannot find the smallest part of the personal weight of Washington in the narrative of his exploits," he declares. Lowell, too, expresses somewhat the same thought in speaking of Washington ("Under the Old Elm," xiii. 82) : —

Such power there is in clear-eyed self-restraint
And purpose clean as light from every selfish taint.

Washington's whole life had been an unconscious preparation for the great part which he was to play. He might have been the model for Lowell's lines ("Epigram," xiii. 271) : —

In life's small things be resolute and great
To keep thy muscles trained: know'st thou when Fate
Thy measure takes, or when she 'll say to thee
"I find thee worthy; do this deed for me "?

Power in one form or another is the thing most desired by all, whether one wish for wealth — to win power over luxuries; for love — to win power over hearts; for fame — to win power over minds; for self-control, — to win power over one's self; that is, to develop character, to acquire reserved force. The man who *can* is the hero. As Emerson says: —

We like people who can do things ("Powers and Laws of Thought," xii. 3).

On the street one day I noticed some workmen trying their best to get a heavy office-table into a narrow hallway and around the curves of some particularly winding stairs. They turned it and twisted it and bungled in every way, but it would not go in. Just then a fashionably dressed gentleman came along. He took in the situation at a glance, and in a moment he was the hero of the day, for he *knew how*. He did not trouble himself to take off his gloves; but as the men lifted the table, he touched it lightly and swung it in the way it should go. Then he watched them as they neared the troublesome turns, and with a wave of his hand he pointed out the one road for that table to take. I doubt whether our hero had ever been a mover of furniture; but in some way, perhaps either as artist or architect or mathematician, he had acquired the power of measuring space with his eye, and, incidentally, of getting that table into its future home. He was a man of reserved power.

Emerson tells an amusing story of another man of such calibre ("Resources," viii. 135), who was captured by some Indians. He heard them say that they meant to scalp him, and he utterly confounded them by offering to save them the trouble and showing them his periwig. "I am a great medicine man," he declared boldly, "and I carry you all in my heart." So he opened his shirt a little and showed to each of the savages in turn the reflection of his own eyeball in a small pocket-mirror which he had hung next to his skin. He poured out a little white brandy, which the Indians supposed to be water, and set fire to it. "If you provoke me," he said quietly, "I will burn up your rivers and your forests." The white man got the best of the red men because he could do what they could not. Maybe the surest way to get the best of any sort of opponent is simply to do better work than he. Emerson says ("Worship," vi. 199):

The way to conquer the foreign artisan is, not to kill him, but to beat his work. . . . The American workman who strikes ten blows with his hammer whilst the foreign workman only strikes one, is as really vanquishing that foreigner as if the blows were aimed at and told on his person.

Reserved force is always in fashion, always a power, but the path is not always clear for its use. More than one obstacle may get into its road; more than one advantage may help to make its way smooth. Even one's manner may make the exercise of power either hard or easy. Emerson says of this ("Manners," iii. 117) : —

Fine manners show themselves formidable to the uncultivated man. They are a subtler science of defence to parry and intimidate. ... Manners aim to facilitate life, to get rid of impediments and bring the man pure to energize. They aid our dealing and conversation as a railway aids travelling, by getting rid of all avoidable obstructions of the road and leaving nothing to be conquered but pure space.

Fine manners arouse an expectation of power. They suggest leisure and ease of mind

13

and a feeling of being perfectly equal to the
occasion. They demand appreciation, even in
advance of any deed that is worthy of it. The
"Autocrat" never wrote a book on etiquette
or an essay on manners, but he has dropped
into his work many a hint that is well worth
heeding. Of one of his table-mates he says
("Over the Teacups," iv. 178) : —

The great trouble is with her voice. It is pitched
a full note too high. It is aggressive, disturbing,
and would wear out a nervous man without his
even knowing what was the matter with him. A
good many crazy Northern people would recover
their reason if they could live for a year or two
among the blacks of the Southern States.

Another quality which would wear out not
only a nervous man but almost any one else
is a companion with what Holmes calls

(*Idem*, 281) "a strong instinctive tendency to contradiction." The most innocent speech arouses its contradictory. If you venture to remark that the walks are dry, you will see the person of a contradictory turn of mind peering down the street to find a puddle. If you "think it may rain to-morrow," your contradicting companion thinks it will not, or else demands "Why?" in such a stand-and-deliver manner that you lose your wits and doubt if there ever was such a thing as rain. You dare not even quote your favorite "What is so rare as a day in June!" lest prompt and decisive the crushing reply should be evoked, "I 've often seen finer days in May." It is with such a companion in mind that Holmes says (*Idem*, 281) : —

Our thoughts are plants that never flourish in inhospitable soils or chilling atmospheres. They are all started under glass, so to speak; that is, sheltered and fastened in our own warm and sunny consciousness. They must expect some rough treatment when you lift the sash from the frame and let the outside elements in upon them. They can bear the rain and the breezes, and be all the better for them; but perpetual contradiction is a pelting hailstorm, which spoils their growth and tends to kill them out altogether.

Holmes is not afraid to touch upon even the smaller details of manners. As he says ("A Rhymed Lesson," xii. 107) : —

Though books on MANNERS are not out of print,
An honest tongue may drop a friendly hint.

.   .   .   .

Do put your accents in the proper spot;
Don't, — let me beg you, — don't say "How?" for
    "What?"

And when you stick on conversation's burs,
Don't strew your pathway with those dreadful *urs*.

Far more seriously than this does Holmes speak of the same matter in "The Autocrat" (page 109). He says : —

What immense conclusions, touching our lives, our fortunes, and our sacred honor, may be reached by means of very insignificant premises. This is eminently true of manners and forms of speech; a movement or a phrase often tells you all you want to know about a person. . . . One of my friends had a marble statuette of Cupid in the parlor of his country-house, bow, arrows, wings, and all complete. A visitor, indigenous to the region, looking pensively at the figure, asked the lady of the house "if that was a statoo of her deceased infant?" What a delicious, though somewhat voluminous biography, special, educational, and æsthetic, in that brief question!

Cheerfulness, too, smooths the way for the exercise of power. Holmes declares ("The Iron Gate," xiii. 204) that he

> Never deemed it sin to gladden
> This vale of sorrows with a wholesome laugh.

In his medical poem, "The Morning Visit" (xii. 143), he gives most substantial advice to be cheery,— and without a doctor's usual fee : —

> And last, not least, in each perplexing case,
> Learn the sweet magic of a *cheerful face;*
> Not always smiling, but at least serene,
> When grief and anguish cloud the anxious scene.
> Each look, each movement, every word and tone,
> Should tell your patient you are all his own;
> Not the mere artist, purchased to attend,
> But the warm, ready, self-forgetting friend,
> Whose genial visit in itself combines
> The best of cordials, tonics, anodynes.

But of all the obstacles in the way of exercising ability, eagerness for praise, for appreciation, for fame, is the most insurmountable. "The reward of work is more work," not a pat on the shoulder. Says Emerson ("Aristocracy," vii. 47): "All spiritual or real power makes its own place. We pass for what we are, and we prosper or fail by what we are." If we are using our best talent according to our best wisdom, what more can we do? Ability cannot be hidden. There are few "mute, inglorious Miltons." Not all our geniuses write poems, however; some of them build bridges, some carry on vast commercial enterprises, some make inventions compared with which the wildest tales of the marvels of fairies and genii are but nursery rhymes. Holmes writes ("Over the Teacups," iv. 114) of "squinting brains," and surely the steadiest man will squint if he tries to fix his brain upon both his work and the praise which he hopes to win. In "The Autocrat" (i. 290) Holmes declares that fame usually comes to those who are thinking about something else, — very rarely to those who say to themselves, "Go to, now, let us be a celebrated individual!" and he adds some remarkably good advice : —

If you have the consciousness of genius, do something to show it. The world is pretty quick, nowadays, to catch the flavor of true originality; if you write anything remarkable, the magazines and newspapers will find you out, as the school-boys find out where the ripe apples and pears are. Produce anything really good, and an intelligent editor will jump at it. Don't flatter yourself that any article of yours is rejected because you are unknown to fame. Nothing pleases an editor more than to get anything worth having from a new hand.

There is no such thing as unappreciated merit.

As much virtue as there is, says Emerson, so much appears; as much goodness as there is, so much reverence it commands. All the devils respect virtue. A man passes for that he is worth. What he is engraves itself on his face, on his form, on his fortunes, in letters of light. Concealment avails him nothing.

So it is that the philosophers and the poets talk to us of living and thinking, of character and its manifestations. Sometimes they return to us only our own well-worn thoughts; but even then it is good to find that another has walked in the same path, to discover that, even without revealing our dilemmas, we have won a friendly sympathy from one who has been in similar troubles. Sometimes, however, they give us wisdom to which we must say, like the little school-girl of the "Psalm of Life," "It is true, but I never thought of it before."

Moreover, just as manners smooth the way for the exercise of power, so may the wording of a thought smooth the way for the thought itself. A well-expressed thought is a nugget, and a nugget of gold is decidedly more convenient to handle and use than the same quantity of the precious metal in solution. The following are some of the nuggets of thought that come from the writers from whom we have already taken so much : —

We put our life into every act.

A man cannot speak but he judges himself.

A friend is a person with whom I may be sincere.

A gentleman makes no noise, a lady is serene.

LIVING AND THINKING

The force of character is cumulative.

Nature encourages no looseness, pardons no errors; freezes punctually at 32°, boils punctually at 212°.

Accuracy is necessary to beauty.

There is always room for a man of force.

Truth is tough. It will not break, like a bubble, at a touch.

In vain we call old notions fudge,
    And bend our conscience to our dealing;
The Ten Commandments will not budge,
    And stealing will continue stealing.

But he is greatest and best who can
Worship Allah by loving man.

Unto gentleness belong
Gifts unknown to pride and wrong.

Nor knowest thou what argument
Thy life to thy neighbor's creed has lent.

Peace that hallows rudest ways.

For there's no rood has not a star above it.

Forbore the ant-hill, shunned to tread
In mercy, on one little head.

And only the sorrow of others
Throws its shadow over me.

That is best which lieth nearest;
Shape from that thy work of art.

This rambling "talk" gives only hints of the wisdom and wit, the poetry and excellence, to be found in the pages of the poets and philosophers. If in these brief quotations you have discovered anything of value, be assured that they are nothing compared with the wealth of the mine from which they were taken, or, to leave the language of figure for that of physics as applied to the homely economics of the household, if there is a flow from the tap, be sure that the source is higher.

ADDITIONAL

EMERSON

Self-Reliance, ii. 43.
Spiritual Laws, ii. 129.
Love, ii. 167.
Friendship, ii. 189.
Prudence, ii. 219.
Heroism, ii. 243.
Greatness, viii. 299.
Natural History of Intellect, xii. 3.
Experience, iii. 43.
Gifts, iii. 157.
Culture, vi. 128.
Beauty, i. 15; vi. 279.
Courage, vii. 251.
Domestic Life, vii. 101.
Aristocracy, x. 31.
Success, vii. 281.
Old Age, vii. 313.
Social Aims, viii. 77.

WHITTIER

Conductor Bradley, i. 359.

LONGFELLOW

The Two Rivers, iii. 234.
The Sifting of Peter, iii. 282.
Nature, iii. 227.
A Shadow, iii. 224.
The Bridge, i. 241.
The Day is Done, i. 246.
The Builders, viii. 305.
Gaspar Becerra, i. 312.
The Singers, i. 320.

HOLMES

Questions for Nineteen or Twenty Centuries Hence, iii. 167.
The Organ-Blower, xiii. 50.
For an Autograph, iv. 177.
Birthday Verses, iii. 176.

QUESTIONS

1. Why does not a poem lose by growing old?
   Because it is new to each new reader.

2. What is the first step toward getting a thing?
   Wishing for it earnestly.

3. What does Emerson say of the possibility
   of reaching your aim?
   *"What will you have?" quoth God; " pay
   for it and take it "* (ii. 91).

4. What does he mean by "dualism"?
   *That there is a gain in every loss and a
   loss in every gain.*

5. What is his idea of wealth?
   The ability to help some one.

6. What does Emerson think is the gain that
   may come from the most severe loss?
   Growth of character.

7. What is character?
   "Reserved force."

8. How is this shown in Washington and other
   great men?
   *Their personal weight is greater than their
   exploits.*

9. What do people desire most?
   Power, in one form or another.

10. What is the noblest form of power?
    Power over one's self, that is, character.

11. What is the surest way to get the better of an opponent?
    To do better work than he.

12. What does Emerson say of fine manners?
    That they are a science of defence and that they clear the way for the exercise of power.

13. What quality does Holmes think would wear any one out?
    "A strong instinctive tendency to contradiction."

14. To what does he compare the effect of "perpetual contradiction" upon thoughts?
    To a pelting hailstorm which "spoils their [plants'] growth and tends to kill them altogether."

15. Why does Holmes declare manners and forms of speech important?

Because they are true exponents of one's education and mode of life, and by them people are judged.

16. What is the most insurmountable obstacle in the way of exercising ability?
    Eagerness for praise or fame.

17. Does Emerson think it possible to conceal power?
    No, he says, "All spiritual or real power makes its own place."

18. In what books of Holmes's may many wise and witty reflections on life be found?
    In the "Breakfast Table" series (i. ii. iii.).

19. Why is it helpful to read the words of poets and philosophers on living and thinking?
    Because they give us either new wisdom or else sympathetic confirmation of our own thoughts.

20. Of the "nuggets of thought" quoted, which seems to you of most practical value?